A Guide to Gemstones
and Rocks

Tagore Ramoutar

First published in 2015.
Copyright © Tagore Ramoutar, Longshot Ventures Ltd 2015.
Published by Longshot Ventures Ltd.

Printed by Lighting Source: ISBN 978-1-907837-86-9
Printed by CreateSpace: ISBN 978-1-907837-87-6
Hardback: ISBN 978-1-907837-88-3

The rights of Tagore Ramoutar to be identified as the author and illustrator of this work has been asserted by him in accordance with the Copyright, Designs and Patents Act, 1988. All rights reserved.

Images not taken by Tagore Ramoutar are reproduced under licence.

Visit our website at www.ericandrufus.com or
www.longshotventures.com

Introduction

As a child I loved rocks and gems, I even had a stone polisher. I always wanted to learn more, however I could never find any good reference books that were written for children.

I am now an adult and have two children who also are fascinated by rocks and gems. In (primary school) year three they both had to do projects on rocks. Again finding good reference books was very difficult.

This book is the book I wish I had as a child and the book that my children wanted when they were investigating rocks for school. I hope you enjoy it.

Contents

Types of Rocks	pages 6-11
Minerals and Gemstones	pages 14-17
Semi-Precious Stones	pages 20-39
Organic Gems/ Other Interesting Stones	pages 42-47
Precious Stones	pages 50-57
Birthstones	pages 60-61
Where to Find Gemstones	pages 64-66

Sedimentary Rocks

Igneous

Metamorphic

Types of Rocks

Types of Rocks

The Earth's crust is made up of rock. Rocks are defined as a solid aggregation of minerals and mineraloids (see page 14). The study of the physical structure of the earth and rocks is called Geology.

There are three main types of rocks: igneous, sedimentary and metamorphic. Their definition's are based on how they are formed.

Igneous (Volcanic)

Igneous rocks are created by magma or lava cooling and becoming solid. Igneous rocks have crystals in them. If magma cools slowly the crystals get big and if it cools quickly the crystals are small. Igneous rocks may also have air bubbles or a glassy surface. Igneous is from a Latin word that means fire.

There are over 700 different types of igneous rocks. Examples of common igneous rocks are granite, basalt, gabbro, obsidian and pumice.

Granite is most commonly used to make tiles.

You will find polished granite tiles in the lobbies of many buildings both as floor tiles and on the walls.

Magma is molten rock. When it cools and solidifies it creates igneous rock.
When magma solidifies slowly underground it creates rocks like granite.
When magma reaches the surface it is called lava. On the surface it solidifies quickly and creates rocks like obsidian and pumice.

Sedimentary (Layered)

Sedimentary rocks are made from material (for example mud/ silt, shells and sand) deposited at the bottom of the sea. Sedimentary rocks may contain fossils, have wavy horizontal lines, layers, grains you can see or be dusty. Sedimentary rocks are usually dull but igneous rocks are shiny.

Examples of common sedimentary rocks include sandstone, mudstone, limestone and chalk.

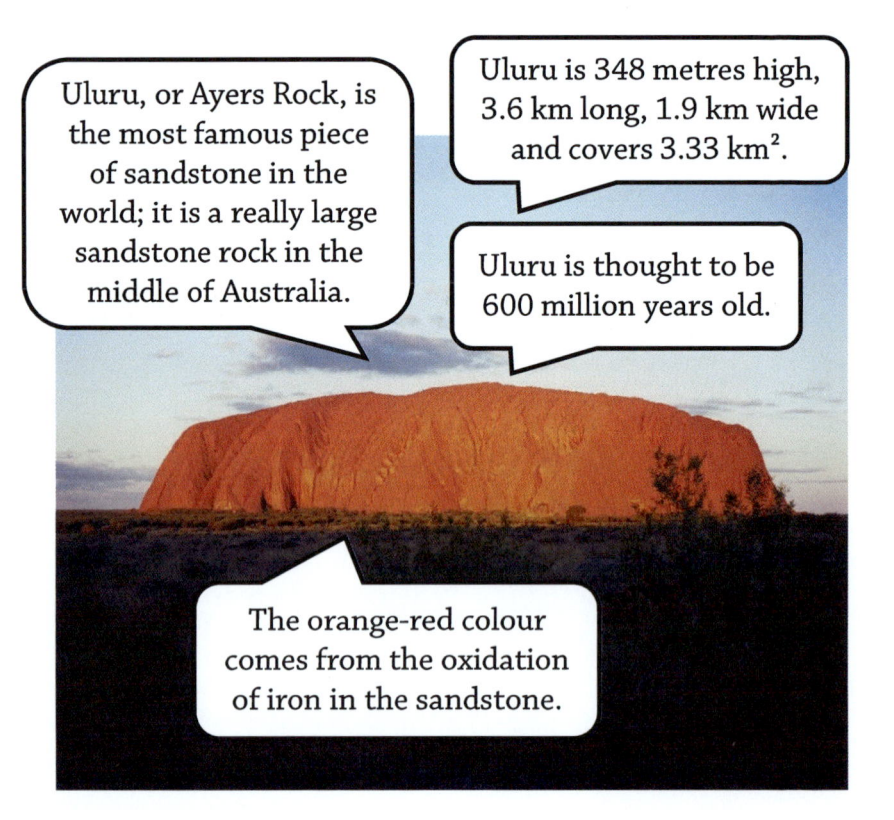

Uluru, or Ayers Rock, is the most famous piece of sandstone in the world; it is a really large sandstone rock in the middle of Australia.

Uluru is 348 metres high, 3.6 km long, 1.9 km wide and covers 3.33 km².

Uluru is thought to be 600 million years old.

The orange-red colour comes from the oxidation of iron in the sandstone.

Sedimentary rocks often have visible layers reflecting the different composition of the deposits.
Sandstone comes in different colours: beige, yellow, brown and red.
Sandstone is often used for building.

Metamorphic (Changed)

Metamorphic rock is made from sedimentary or igneous rocks that have been changed by extreme heat or pressure. They are formed either by pressure deep under the Earth's crust, extreme heat from volcanic magma or by the intense collisions and friction of tectonic plates. Metamorphic is from a Greek word meaning change.

Examples of metamorphic rocks include anthracite (coal), quartzite, marble, slate, granulite, gneiss and schist. Marble is a metamorphic rock formed from the sedimentary rock limestone. Slate is a metamorphic rock formed from mudstone.

One of the most famous buildings in the world is made entirely from marble. The Taj Mahal in India was built by Mughal Emperor Shah Jahan in memory of his wife, Mumtaz Mahal in 1653.

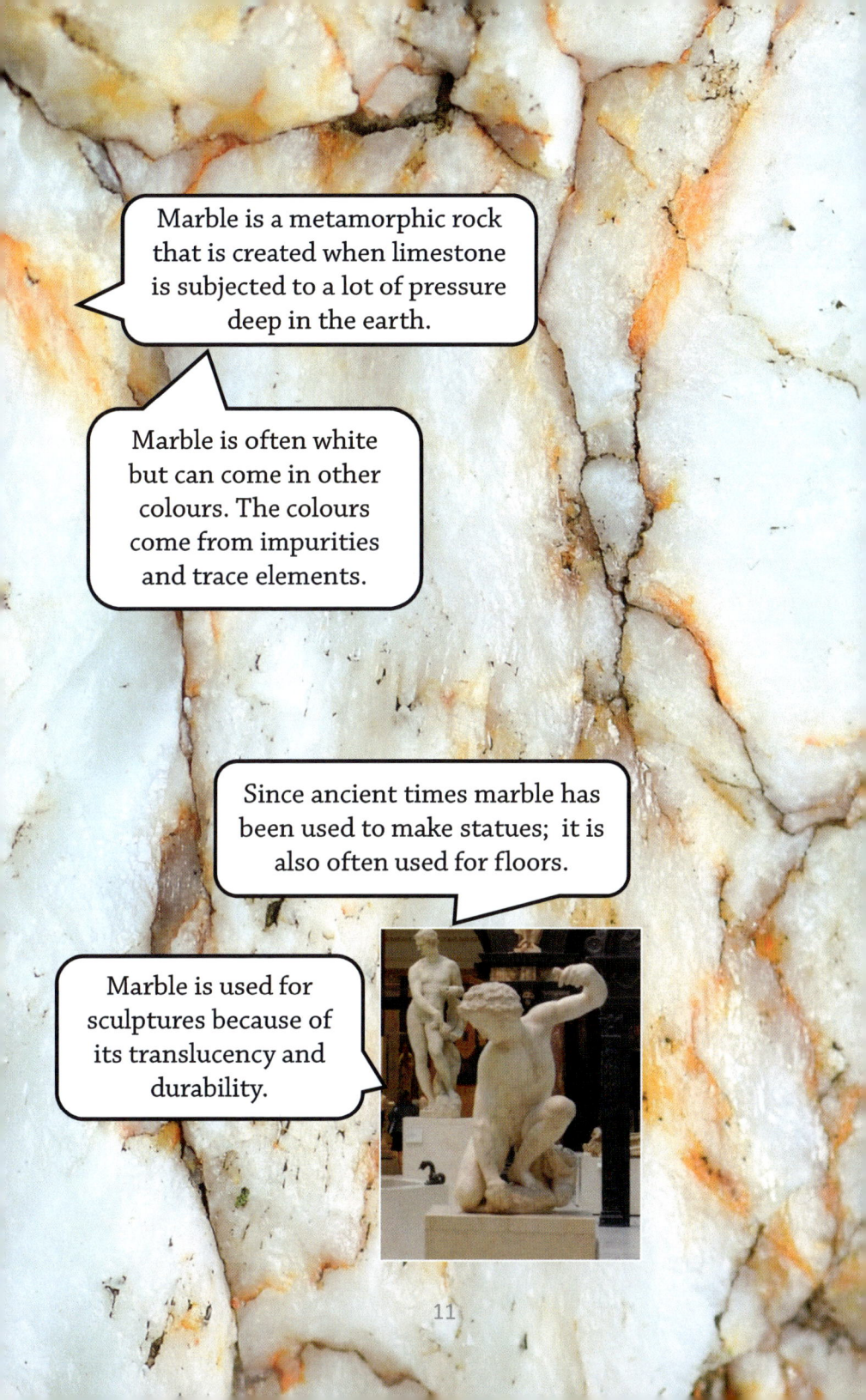

Marble is a metamorphic rock that is created when limestone is subjected to a lot of pressure deep in the earth.

Marble is often white but can come in other colours. The colours come from impurities and trace elements.

Since ancient times marble has been used to make statues; it is also often used for floors.

Marble is used for sculptures because of its translucency and durability.

Semi-Precious

Minerals

Gemstones

Precious

Minerals and Gemstones

What are Minerals and Mineraliods

Minerals are naturally occurring substances formed deep in the Earth by geological processes. They are solid and have a crystal structure. Minerals can be just one chemical element but are usually a compound of more than one chemical element.

Minerals are "crystalline" - they have an ordered atomic structure. Mineraloids are "amorphous" - their internal atomic structure is not ordered and so do not have well formed crystals. A mineraloid is defined "as an amorphous, naturally occurring, inorganic solid that does not exhibit crystallinity".

To be a mineral, a material must meet five requirements: it must be naturally occurring; inorganic; solid; have an ordered atomic structure; and have a defined chemical composition.

There are over 4000 different types of minerals, but only about 30 of these are commonly found in the Earth's crust. Minerals are not rocks, they are the components of rocks (combined together minerals form rocks). Some examples of minerals are feldspar, quartz, calcite, gypsum, pyrite, gold and diamond.

Some examples of mineraloids are opal, pumice and obsidian.

Gemstones are semi-precious and precious crystals (minerals) that are used for jewellery. Some rocks (such as lapis lazuli) and organic materials that are not minerals (such as amber or jet), are also used for jewellery; and are therefore also classed as gemstones. Generally stones are classed as gemstones if they are prized for their appearance and / or rarity.

How Gemstones are Formed

Today's gemstones were formed millions of years ago deep in the crust of the Earth by the extreme heat found at the core. Gemstones were then subsequently brought to the surface /near to the surface by volcanic eruptions. Gemstones are either igneous (and crystalline) or metamorphic.

Crystalline gemstones, such as quartz, amethyst and agate, were formed when liquid silica (quartz) cooled in cavities of igneous rocks. Slow cooling of the liquid silica allows impurities to settle into coloured bands on the outside and crystals in centre. You can see this in stones called "geodes" which when split have coloured layers of agate and beautiful crystals in the centre. The most well known geode based gemstones are agate and amethyst.

Geode

Agate

Metamorphic gemstones are formed when mixtures of minerals undergo heat and pressure deep in the Earth. The mixtures create the colours and flecks in the rocks. At very high temperatures complex crystalline rocks or gemstones such as garnet are formed.

Crystal gems are made up of atoms in a regular pattern called a lattice. The distinctive shapes of different crystals are caused by the different shapes of these lattices of atoms. The different colours of crystals are caused by atoms of another element being included in the lattice. For example rubies and emeralds are both varieties of the mineral corundum (aluminium oxide) with different impurities; rubies have chromium in the lattice and blue sapphires have both iron and titanium.

Using Gemstones (cutting and polishing)

Most gemstones are cut and polished for use in jewellery. Different gemstones bend light in different ways. Each stone needs to be cut differently to maximise their brilliance (sparkle). Great skill and care is taken to cut each gem. There are two main classifications of cutting: "cabochons" (stones cut as smooth, dome shaped) and "faceted stones" (cut with a faceting machine by polishing small flat facets at regular intervals at set angles).

Some semi-precious gemstones are not cut but are polished by tumbling in a stone polisher. They are tumbled with abrasive powders until smooth and then washed to give a sheen – these are know as "baroques".

Different Types of Gemstones

There are over 130 minerals and other natural materials used as gemstones. Below is a list of the main ones; in the following pages there are details about some of the more well known gemstones (the ones covered are in bold).

Andalusite	**Garnet**	Vesuvianite
Axinite	Hessonite	Xenotime
Benitoite	*Hambergite*	Zeolite (Thomsonite)
Beryl	*Hematite*	**Zircon**
Aquamarine	**Jade**	Zoisite
Bixbite	*Jadeite*	*Tanzanite*
Emerald	*Nephrite*	*Thulite*
Morganite	Kornerupine	
Bloodstone	Kunzite	
Cassiterite	Malachite	
Celestite	Peridot	
Chrysoberyl	Prehnite	
Alexandrite	Pyrite	
Cat's Eye	**Quartz**	
Chrysocolla	**Amethyst**	
Chrysoprase	*Citrine*	
Clinohumite	***Smoky Quartz***	
Cordierite	***Tiger's-eye***	
Corundum	***Chalcedony***	
Ruby	***Agate***	
Sapphire	***Carnelian***	
Danburite	***Jasper***	
Diamond	*Aventurine*	
Diopside	*Onyx*	
Dioptase	Rhodochrosite	
Dumortierite	Spinel	
Feldspar	Sugilite	
Amazonite	**Topaz**	
Labradorite	**Turquoise**	
Moonstone	Tourmaline	
Sunstone	Variscite	

Other materials are also used as gems.

Organic materials:
Amber
Ammolite
Bone
Copal
Coral (precious)
Ivory
Jet
Nacre /Mother of pearl
Pearl

Inorganic mineraloids:
Obsidian
Opal

Other rocks:
Lapis lazuli
Maw sit sit
Unakite

Amethyst

Calcite

Carnelian

Tiger's Eye

Semi-Precious Stones

Feldspars
The Most Common Mineral

Feldspars are a silicate, they are a family of minerals consisting of aluminium, oxygen and silicon plus other trace elements. They are the most common mineral on Earth, making up approximately 60% of the crust.

The name feldspar comes from the German word "Feldspat", meaning "field" and "a rock that does not contain ore".

Feldspars are formed from cooling magma and are the major component of most igneous rocks, but are also found in metamorphic rocks and even in sedimentary rocks. Feldspar is found in granite, where it varies in colour from pink to grey.

Feldspar is more commonly used for industrial purposes rather than as gemstones. It is used in glassmaking, ceramics and as a filler in paints, plastics and rubber.

There are four main gemstones in the feldspar family amazonite, moonstone, sunstone and labradorite.

Amazonite is named after green stones originally found in the Amazon Basin, however there are no known deposits of amazonite found there.

It is found in Russia, US, Madagascar and other areas of Brazil. The blue green colour comes from microscopic traces of lead and water in the feldspar.

Amazonite is known as the stone of courage and truth.

Moonstone

Moonstone is the most well known gemstone from the feldspar family. Moonstones get their name from the bluish white spots within them; when you move a moonstone they shimmer. Traditionally moonstones are white but you can get beige, yellow, green, blue sheen, greyish and pink varieties.

The beauty of moonstone is usually only visible when they are cut. Classically they are cut as cabochons, the depth of the stone reveals the internal light shimmer.

In Ancient Roman times it was thought that "moonstone changed in appearance with the phases of the moon" and that the image of Diana, goddess of the moon, was enclosed within it.

Moonstones were traditionally believed to bring victory, health and wisdom to those who wore them. In India moonstone is considered a sacred stone and is believed to bring good fortune. Moonstone is the birthstone of June.

The main source of moonstones is Sri Lanka, but deposits are also found in Australia, Austria, Mexico, Madagascar, Burma, Norway, Poland, India and USA.

Moonstones have "silvery rays [that] glint like moonbeams over water".

Moonstones are also known as adularia (due to them being found in Adula in the Alps).

Quartz

Quartz is the second most common mineral in the Earth's crust (after feldspar). It is made up of a continuous framework of silicon–oxygen in a tetrahedra pattern.

$$\begin{array}{c}\text{O}^-\quad\quad\text{O}^-\\|\quad\quad\quad|\\-\text{O}\cdots\text{Si}-\text{O}-\text{Si}\cdots\text{O}^-\\|\quad\quad\quad|\\-\text{O}\quad\quad\text{O}^-\end{array}$$

Many of the most common semi-precious stones are varieties of quartz; such as rose quartz, agates, amethyst, carnelian, citrine, tiger's eye and even chalcedony. Since ancient times quartz has been used to make jewellery.

Quartz is found in granite and other igneous rocks, but it is also found in sedimentary rocks, such as sandstone, and metamorphic rocks. Whenever you see that little clear crystal shine in a rock it is probably quartz.

Most quartz in the Earth's crust is microscopic / very small but crystals can grow to several metres long.

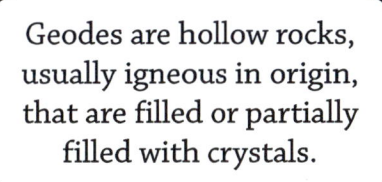

Geodes are hollow rocks, usually igneous in origin, that are filled or partially filled with crystals.

Quartz often forms inside geodes. They have an inner layer of crystalline quartz and an outer layer of chalcedony or banded agate.

You can often buy sections of geodes in rock shops.

Quartz is the hardest common mineral. Only rarer minerals, such as diamonds, are harder.

The Main Quartz Gemstones

There are many varieties of quartz and they make up some of the most popular gemstones:

Chalcedony*	Micro crystalline quartz and moganite mixture (white or lightly coloured).
Agate*	Multi-coloured, banded chalcedony, semi-translucent to translucent.
Onyx	Agate where the bands are straight, parallel and consistent in size.
Jasper*	Opaque, typically red to brown.
Aventurine	Translucent chalcedony with small shimmering inclusions.
Tiger's eye*	Stripy gold to red-brown.
Rock crystal	Clear, colourless.
Amethyst*	Purple, transparent.
Citrine	Yellow to reddish orange to brown, greenish yellow.
Prasiolite	Mint green, transparent.
Rose quartz*	Pink, translucent.
Rutilated quartz	Has needle-like inclusions of rutile.
Milky quartz	White, translucent to opaque.
Smoky quartz*	Brown to grey, opaque. Also know as cairngorm.
Carnelian*	Reddish orange chalcedony, translucent.

* Means there are more details on the following pages

Chalcedony

Chalcedony is the most common form of quartz consisting of micro-crystal silica made up of quartz and moganite. Chalcedony is found in igneous rocks, metamorphic rocks and even sedimentary rocks. Chalcedony is a name given to many different gemstones as well as to the chalcedony stone itself. Chalcedony occurs in a wide range of varieties, some of the most well known are: agate, aventurine, carnelian, chrysoprase, bloodstone, moss agate, tree agate, mtorolite and onyx.

Chalcedony has a waxy lustre and is either semi-transparent or translucent. It is most often white to grey, greyish-blue or can be a shade of brown ranging from pale to nearly black.

Chalcedony has been used since the Bronze Age.

Chalcedony is probably the most common gemstone and is found in most countries. Typically it is used for making beads / inexpensive jewellery.

Chalcedony is named after an Ancient Greek town called Chalkedon.

Chalcedony rocks are one of the earliest materials used by humans. It was used for cutting tools, arrowheads, bowls and cups.

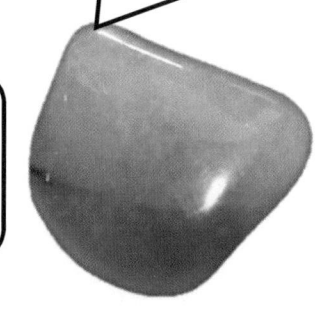

Agate

Agates are a banded or layered form of chalcedony and crystalline quartz; they are formed in nodules of volcanic rock. The agate family has many different varieties, some of the more common are below:

Agate Geode	Outer layer of agate in a geode.
Blue Lace Agate	Agate with light blue bands in a lacy or wavy pattern.
Botswana Agate	Agate banded with fine parallel lines of white, purple or peach from Botswana.
Condor Agate	Vivid coloured agate from Argentina.
Crazy Lace Agate	Agate with twisting and turning bands of various colours.
Eye Agate	Agate with banded, concentric rings that are perfectly rounded.
Fortification Agate	Agate with a pattern of connecting bands which look like a medieval castle.
Iris Agate	Iridescent agate with spectral colours on a translucent colourless or white base.
Laguna Agate	A colourful agate with very dense banding from Ojo Laguna, Mexico.
Sagenite Agate	Agate with hair like inclusions arranged in fans or bursts.
Sardonyx	Agate with parallel bands of brown or red alternating with white or black bands.
Snakeskin Agate	Agate with a scale-like layer that resembles snakeskin; also a reddish brown agate with small black concentric bands.

Agate
(Blue Lace Agate)

Agates are generally found in igneous rocks and sometimes in metamorphic rocks. They are formed in cavities, cracks or even fossils in old volcanic rocks and lavas. The agate nodules form in the cavities in the rock as siliceous matter/ gelatinous silica in percolating water is deposited in layers (the layers that later form the agate).

The first deposit forms the skin that is either dark greenish or a brown rusty colour. The layers are built up but often don't fully fill the cavity, with the last deposit usually being crystal quartz.

Agates are extremely resistant to weathering and remain as nodules or geodes even after the original rock has become eroded. Hence agates are often found in the soil, or in gravel beds in streams and along the shore.

Agates are found all over the world, but particularly in: Africa, Brazil, Egypt, Germany, Morocco, Czech Republic, Italy, India, Mexico, Nepal, USA and the UK. Blue lace agate comes from Namibia and South Africa.

Blue lace agate is named "blue lace" because the bands are thought to look like lace.

Agate is the birthstone for the Zodiac sign of Gemini.

Blue lace agate is one of the most popular and well known types of agate.

Jasper

Jasper is an aggregate (combination) of micro-quartz, chalcedony and other minerals. The colour differences come from the minerals and the patterns come from mineral infilling along fractures created when the stone was originally formed.

Jasper is most commonly red (due to iron), but also comes in yellow, brown, green and even very rarely blue. The colours come from the differing mineral contents of the original sediments or volcanic ash that have created the gemstone.

Jasper breaks with a smooth surface and can be highly polished and so has been used for ornaments and jewellery since ancient times.

Jasper is common and found worldwide, but major deposits are found in India, Russia, Kazakhstan, Indonesia, Egypt, Madagascar, Australia, Brazil, Venezuela, Uruguay and USA.

Jasper means "spotted or speckled stone" and comes from the Old French "jaspre".

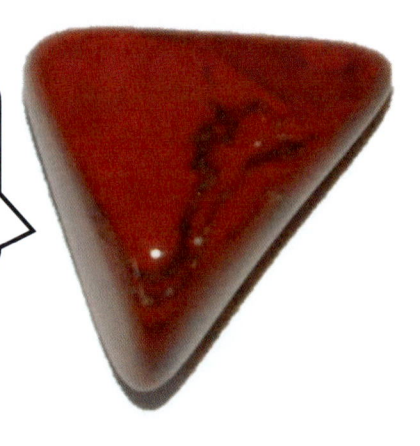

Tiger's Eye

Tiger's eye is a form of chalcedony. It is a metamorphic stone that started as a fibrous blue mineral called crocidolite (also known as asbestos). Under pressure deep in the Earth crocidolite gradually transforms into fibrous quartz; either a blue stone called hawk's eye or tiger's eye. Tiger's eye is of course named for the likeness to real tiger's eyes. It comes in colours from yellow to brown to red.

The transformation creates parallel lines within the gem which in turn gives the shifting play of light that characterises tiger's eye.

Tiger's eye has a silky lustre / reflectance that is known as chatoyance. The stripes in the stone reflect the light. The effect is named after the French for "cat's eye".

Tiger's eye is found in South Africa, India, Myanmar, Sri Lanka, Australia, Brazil, USA, Namibia, Canada, China, Korea and Spain.

Some tiger's eye stones are attracted to magnets because they contain magnetite.

Roman soldiers wore tiger's eye for protection in battle.

Amethyst

Amethyst is a purple / violet type of quartz. It is found in geodes and can have huge flawless crystals. It is very popular for use in jewellery and is the birthstone for February. The purple colour of amethyst is thought to be caused by iron impurities or by exposure to natural radiation. The purple colour of an amethyst may occasionally fade over time if exposed to strong light. They are also sensitive to high heat; if heated to over 400°C the colour of amethyst changes to brownish-yellow or red or sometimes green.

The name amethyst comes from the Ancient Greek "amethystos", which means "not drunken". Amethyst was believed to cure drunkenness. The Tibetans consider amethyst to be sacred to the Buddha. In Christianity it symbolises celibacy and is worn by Bishops.

Amethyst is found in Brazil (Brazil is the largest producer in the world), Uruguay, Argentina, Bolivia, Mexico, South Korea, Austria, Russia, India, Namibia, Madagascar, Zambia, USA, Canada and in small quantities in the UK.

In the Middle Ages amethyst was believed to bring victory in battle and to protect the wearer from sorcery.

Rose Quartz

Rose quartz is one of the most common varieties of the quartz family. It has a delicate pink rose colour (you can get it in pale pink to rose red). The colour comes from trace amounts of titanium, iron, manganese or dumortierite in the silicon dioxide crystal. It is often found in massive blocks within pegmatite deposits (an igneous rock).

Rose quartz is often used for carving, in brooches or beads in necklaces and bracelets. It is often cut as cabochons, hearts or tumbled.

Rose quartz is the stone of love and is called the "Love Stone" or "Heart Stone". It is also used by crystal healers.

Rose quartz is found all over the world in pegmatite deposits. It is commercially mined in Madagascar, South Africa, Namibia and USA (South Dakota).

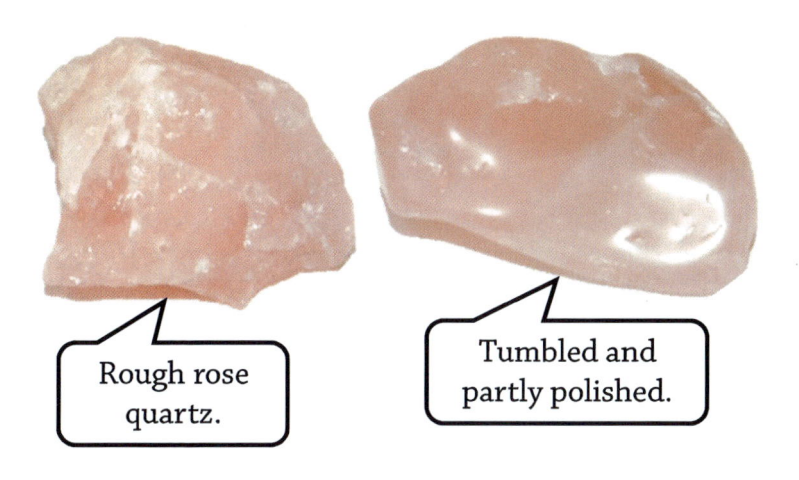

Rough rose quartz.

Tumbled and partly polished.

Carnelian
(also spelled cornelian)

Carnelian is an orange brownish-red mineral gemstone that is a variety of the silica mineral chalcedony. The beautiful orangey colour comes from impurities of iron oxide. Carnelian is translucent, and may contain lighter, darker and cloudy areas within an individual stone.

In ancient times carnelian was a very valued gemstone. In Roman times it was engraved and used on seal rings / signet rings.

It is most commonly found in Brazil, India, Uruguay, Siberia, USA and Germany; it can also be found in the UK.

Roman's used carved carnelian for imprinting wax seals, because wax does not stick to carnelian.

Carnelian is the birthstone for July.

Bloodstone

Bloodstone is sometimes called heliotrope or blood jasper. It is a dark green variety of chalcedony that is speckled with red or brown spots. The spots look similar to blood stains, hence its name, they are formed by iron oxide impurities. Bloodstones often have uneven colour and the spots can even rarely be yellow, if yellow they are referred to as plasma rather than blood. The green colour is caused by dense inclusions of chlorite or amphibole minerals inside the chalcedony.

Legend has it that bloodstone was formed during the crucifixion of Jesus Christ. A Roman soldier thrust his spear into Christ's side and drops of blood fell onto pieces of green jasper lying below the cross; and bloodstone was created.

Bloodstone is found in India, Madagascar, Brazil, China, Australia, Germany Russia and in the Hebrides, UK.

Bloodstone is one of the birthstones for March.

Jade

Jade is an umbrella term used to describe two different metamorphic rocks, nephrite and jadeite. The minerals look alike and have similar physical properties. Jade is traditionally a green stone but can come in other colours. The deeper the colour green the more valuable the jade; the most valuable form is called "Imperial Jade", it is translucent emerald-green.

Nephrite is slightly softer and can get scratched. Jadeite is more vulnerable to chipping.

Jade is very much associated with China, but has also been an important gemstone in Ancient India and Latin America.

Nephrite is more common and jadeite is now more rare. The main source of jadeite is Myanmar (it is also the only source of imperial jade); jadeite is also found in Japan, Canada, Guatemala, Kazakhstan, Russia, Turkey, Cuba and USA. Nephrite is found in New Zealand, Australia, Brazil, China, Canada, Zimbabwe, Russia, Taiwan, Alaska and Poland.

Nephrite makes a musical tone when hit; jadeite doesn't.

The Jain temple of Kolanpak, India, is home to the world's largest sculpture made from a single jade rock (1.5m high sculpture).

Turquoise

Turquoise is an opaque blue green "turquoise" gemstone. It is an aluminium phosphate containing copper. Turquoise almost never forms crystals visible to the naked eye and is known as a cryptocrystalline mineral (very very minute crystals). The blue colour is due to copper and green from iron impurities. It is typically found in very arid (dry) regions.

The name "turquoise" dates from the 16th century and comes from the French "turqueise", meaning "Turkish stone", because although it was mined in Persia (now called Iran) it came to Europe via Turkey. The colour turquoise was named after this gemstone.

Turquoise was historically prized in Persia, Egypt and also Native American civilisations, particularly the Aztecs. It was used for jewellery and decoration.

Iran and the Sinai Peninsula have been an important source of turquoise for over 2000 years. It is also found in the USA, China, Afghanistan, Australia, India, Chile, Germany, Mexico, Turkestan and in small quantities in Cornwall in the UK.

The Ancient Egyptians thought blue symbolised regeneration.

King Tutankhamen's funeral mask is inlaid with turquoise.

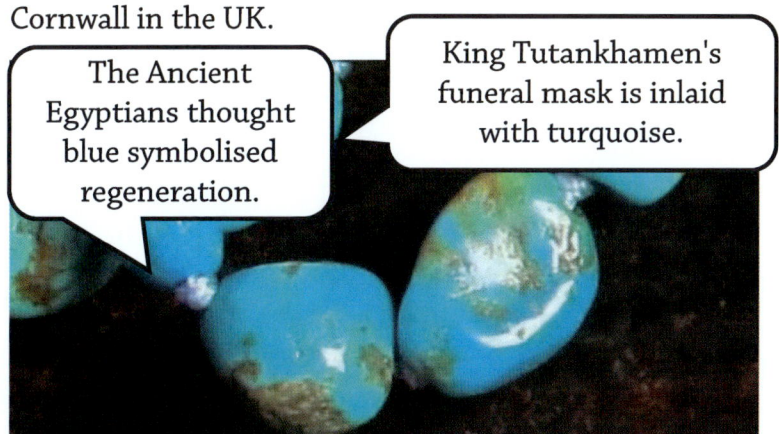

Other Gemstones Found in the UK

There are 15 different types of gemstone found in the UK (see pages 64-65 for details of which ones and where they are found). Most have been covered already but there are six that haven't: cairngorm (or smoky quartz, a variety of quartz), garnet, kyanite, serpentine, topaz and zircon.

Cairngorm/Smoky Quartz

Cairngorm is a variety of smoky quartz; it comes from the Cairngorm Mountains in Scotland. It is a silicon dioxide (quartz) crystal, with the smoky effect coming from "free" silicon and colour from iron oxide impurities. Smoky quartz is grey to brownish grey translucent quartz gemstone.

Cairngorm usually has a smoky yellow-brown colour, though may be occasionally be a grey-brown.

> Cairngorm is used in traditional Scottish jewellery and as decoration on kilt pins.

> The largest cairngorm crystal is kept at Braemar Castle and weighs 23.6 kg.

Garnet

Garnet is the name of a group of related silicate minerals that have similar physical properties and crystal forms but different chemical compositions. The name is generally given to six different varieties, of which almandine and pyrope are most commonly used as gemstones. Garnets come in many colours but are most well known as being dark red.

Garnet is the birthstone of January.

Rough garnets.

Red garnets were the most common gemstones in Ancient Roman world.

Kyanite

Kyanite is a metamorphic gemstone, that is not well known or widely used. It is usually greyish or blue but can be colourless, white, green, yellow or even orange.

It is a strange stone which is softer on the long side of the crystal and harder on the short side of the crystal.

Serpentine

Serpentine is a group of around 20 minerals that are made up of hydrated magnesium silicate. Serpentines are a metamorphic mineral and are green, yellowish-green or brownish-green colour.

The name serpentine comes from the Latin serpentinus, meaning "serpent rock".

Topaz

Topaz is a silicate mineral containing aluminium and fluoride. While pure topaz is colourless, it is usually coloured by impurities; the most prized colour is golden orange-yellow. The most common colour now-a-days is blue topaz but this is almost always created artificially by heat treating and irradiating other colours of topaz.

Topaz is found in igneous rocks such as granite and rhyolite. It can form exceptionally large flawless crystals. Some of the biggest cut topaz gemstones have weighed thousands of carats (see page 56 for definition of carats).

Topaz is the birthstone of November.

Golden yellow orange topaz is called "Imperial Topaz".

Zircon

Zircon is a ubiquitous mineral found in some of the oldest rocks in the world. It is found in igneous rocks (such as granite), in many metamorphic rocks and in sedimentary rocks (such as sandstone). It is also found as one of the constituents of beach sand in Australia, India, Brazil, and Florida.

Zircon is a zirconium silicate ($ZrSiO_4$); it is usually in micro crystal form but it can form 1 cm+ large crystals. Zircon varies in colour from colourless, yellow-golden, red, brown, blue to green. Colourless zircon gems are sometimes used as a substitute for diamonds and are called "Matura diamonds".

The colour of zircons can be changed by heat. In nature the development of pink, red and purple zircon is thought to occur after hundreds of millions of years of heating at 350°C. In laboratories common brown zircons can be changed to colourless and blue zircons by heating to above 800°C.

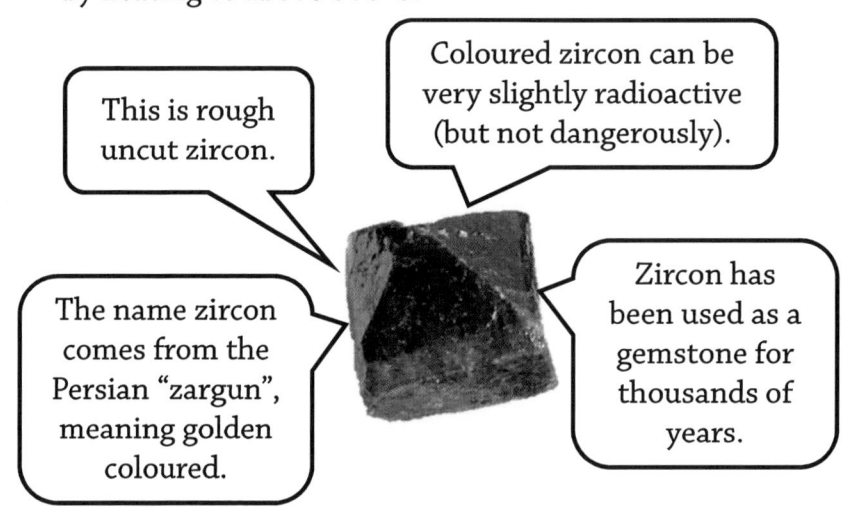

This is rough uncut zircon.

Coloured zircon can be very slightly radioactive (but not dangerously).

The name zircon comes from the Persian "zargun", meaning golden coloured.

Zircon has been used as a gemstone for thousands of years.

Amber

Pearl

Calcite

Pyrite

Organic Gems/ Other Interesting Rocks

Organic Gems
Amber

Amber is an organic yellow orange gemstone (though you can get a blue version from the Dominican Republic). It is formed from fossilized/ hardened tree resin (not sap) from ancient evergreen trees. Amber is formed from sticky resin that hardens over centuries. Typically amber contains organic matter that got stuck before the hardening, it sometimes includes fossilized insects especially mosquitoes.

Amber can be transparent, though it is often cloudy and translucent. The cloudiness is generally caused by trapped air bubbles.

The world's biggest amber deposits are in the Baltic Sea near Kaliningrad, Russia; plus on the coast of Latvia and Lithuania. In addition amber is found on the Baltic coast of Poland, around Gdansk. Amber is very light and is often found washed up on beaches after storms.

The Dominican Republic is the other significant source of amber, including blue amber. Other more minor sources of amber are Germany, Italy (Sicily), Myanmar, Mexico, Canada, USA and even the UK.

This is raw amber from the coast of Kaliningrad, on the Baltic Sea.

Organic Gems
Pearls

Pearls are organic gemstones that are formed inside living molluscs, such as oysters and mussels. Pearls are made up from calcium carbonate and organic conchiolin deposited in concentric layers. Pearls occur naturally in the wild, both in the sea (saltwater pearls) and rivers (freshwater pearls).

Natural saltwater pearls are very rare and are very expensive. They take around three years to form and only one in several hundred have them. It is thought that they form when a microscopic object gets trapped inside. Inside the shell is also made up of the same material and is called nacre or "mother of pearl".

Most pearls used today are cultured pearls. They are formed by putting a "foreign object" inside an oyster to promote the growth of pearl around it. These can be mass produced in warm waters, around volcanic atolls or in lagoons. Each oyster can produce 1-3 pearls.

Freshwater pearls are even more abundant, they come from mussels and each mussel can make up to 50 pearls. Freshwater pearls are generally not round and are cheaper.

The best pearls are round.

Calcite

Calcite is a pretty, relatively soft, carbonate mineral that is often collected or is used in earrings and pendants. It is a stable form of calcium carbonate and is one of the most common minerals on earth. Pure calcite is colourless, but calcite is usually coloured due to impurities and can come in many different colours.

Calcite is common in sedimentary rocks, particularly limestone and chalk as well as being the main mineral in marble. It also occurs in caverns as stalactites* (hang from the ceiling) and stalagmites (come from the floor).

Calcite can form visible crystals that are transparent to opaque. Calcite sometimes exhibits fluorescence and can fluoresce pink under long wave ultraviolet light and blue under short wave ultraviolet light.

Calcite can come in many different colours.

The two largest single crystals of calcite weighed approx 250 tons and were 7×7×2m and 6×6×3m. They were found in Iceland.

- One way to remember which is which is "tights fall down" and the word stalactites has "tites" in it.

Iron Pyrite (Fools Gold)

Iron pyrite is a metallic pale yellow mineral that is also known as "fool's gold". It is an iron sulfide with the chemical formula FeS_2. Pyrite usually forms cuboid crystals. Pyrite has a metallic lustre and colour that can fool people into thinking it is gold, hence the nickname "fool's gold".

The name "pyrite" comes from Ancient Greek and means "of fire" or "in fire". The name was given to several types of stones that create sparks when struck with steel.

Pyrite is found with other sulfides or oxides in quartz veins, coal beds, sedimentary rock and metamorphic rock. Very occasionally it is found with small quantities of gold.

Fool's gold sparks when it is struck with a hard object.

In the 16th and 17th century pyrite was used in early guns to ignite the gunpowder.

Iron pyrite is unstable and can decompose if exposed to air and water.

Flint

Flint is a hard, sedimentary form of mineral quartz. It is a form chalcedony from the sub-family of rocks called chert. Flint is the name given to chert found as nodules or masses in the chalk or limestone.

Flint is usually found in nodules (they look like pebbles) that are dark grey, black, greenish, white or brown in colour on the inside and covered with a thin white rough layer on the outside. The inside rock has a glassy or waxy appearance and is very hard. The properties of the inside rock are what makes it so special. Whilst being very hard it can be fractured or flaked into sharp edged pieces.

Flint is one of the most important rocks in human history and is irrevocably connected with early human development. It has been used to make sharp stone tools for at least two million years.

Later flint was also used to make fire; as when it strikes steel it creates a spark. It has even been used to build houses.

When broken flint feels very smooth.

Flint has been used for making tools since the Stone Age.

Flint is very hard but can be flaked to make sharp edges.

Flint was used for making tools 1.4 million years ago in Spain.

It has been used to make axes, knives and arrow heads.

This is an arrow head.

A flint axe found in Norfolk, and dating from between 550,000 and 700,000 years ago, is thought to be the oldest man-made object ever found in Britain. You can see it in the British Museum.

Sapphires

Rubies

Emeralds

Diamonds

Precious Stones

Precious Stones

Today there are four types of gemstone that are classed as "precious": diamond, ruby, sapphire and emerald. This is primarily due to their rarity. Some people also class pearl and opal as precious.

Corundum

Ruby and sapphire are both types of corundum, which is an aluminium oxide mineral. Corundum is a very hard, tough, and stable mineral; it is the hardest mineral after diamond. Ruby and sapphire are actually the same mineral but just different colours. Ruby is the red variety, and sapphire is generally the blue variety though you can get sapphires in other colours.

Sapphire is the birthstone of September.

Cornflower blue is the most valuable of the sapphire colours. Sapphires come from Sri Lanka, Myanmar, Thailand, Cambodia, Madagascar, Tanzania, Australia, and USA. The Kashmir region of India/Pakistan used to be famous for its Kashmir-blue Sapphire.

Ruby is the birthstone of July; it represents love, health and wisdom. The red colour of ruby is usually caused by tiny inclusions of chromium. The most valuable rubies are from Myanmar, but they also come from Thailand, Madagascar, Sri Lanka, India, Cambodia, Vietnam, Australia, Tanzania, Mozambique, Afghanistan, Pakistan, Tajikstan and USA.

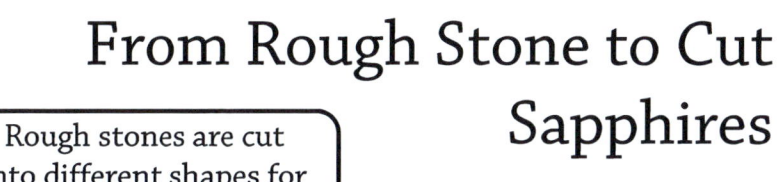

From Rough Stone to Cut Sapphires

Rough stones are cut into different shapes for use in jewellery.

Sapphires come in lots of colours, but blue is the most well known colour.

Emeralds

Emeralds are a precious stone variety of the mineral beryl, they are green due to trace elements of chromium and sometimes vanadium. They are highly prized because of their beautiful intense dark green colour. The name emerald comes from the Ancient Greek "smaragdos" via the Old French 'esmeralde' meaning green gemstone.

Emeralds are one of the oldest gemstones in the world with some being 2600 million years old. The process of creating emeralds tends to have created flaws including fissures and bubbles; the fewer flaws the higher the value.

Emeralds have been mined for a long time; with mining in Egypt being recorded as long ago as 3000 BC. South America is most associated with emeralds with the Incas and Aztecs regarding them as holy stones. The Vedas (Ancient Indian holy books) say "Emeralds promise good luck" and "The emerald enhances the well-being". Pliny (the Roman philosopher) said "that green gladdened the eye without tiring it".

Many of the best emeralds are from Colombia, but fine emeralds also come from Zambia, Brazil, Zimbabwe, Madagascar, Pakistan, India, Afghanistan and Russia. In addition they can be found in Australia, Austria, Bulgaria, Cambodia, Canada, China, Egypt, Ethiopia, France, Germany, Italy, Kazakhstan, Mozambique, Namibia, Nigeria, Norway, Somalia, South Africa, Spain, Switzerland, Tanzania and USA.

The best emeralds are from Columbia. Columbia produces around 50% of all emeralds.

Top quality emeralds without imperfections are very rare and therefore can be worth more than diamonds.

Emeralds weigh less than diamonds.

Emeralds were first mined in Ancient Egypt. One of Cleopatra's favourite stones was an emerald.

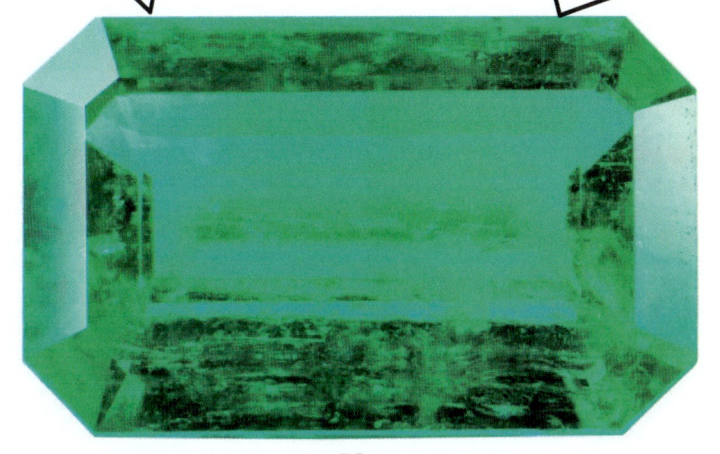

Diamonds

Diamonds are the most precious stones in the world. They are the hardest natural substance on Earth, and can only be scratched by another diamond. The word diamond comes from the Greek word "adamas" which means invincible, indestructible or unbreakable.

Diamonds were formed billions of years ago deep in the Earth. They have been carried to the Earth's surface by old volcanic eruptions. Diamonds are made of a single element, carbon. Diamonds are created around 100 miles below ground where the carbon experiences temperatures of 1000-1600°C and immense pressure; the carbon then bonds in a strong, tetrahedral structure to create diamond.

Diamonds have been desired and valued thousands of years. The first diamonds are believed to have been found in India in 500 BC. Until the 18th century, the only diamond mines were in India. The Ancient Hindus believed that diamonds could protect their wearers from danger. In fact many ancient cultures believed that diamonds gave the wearer strength and courage during battle.

The Ancient Romans and Greeks believed that diamonds were the tears of the gods or splinters from falling stars. In the first century AD, the Roman philosopher Pliny said "Diamond is the most valuable, not only of precious stones, but of all things in this world".

In 1725, diamonds were discovered in South America and then in 1840s diamonds were also discovered in North America. Then in the late 1800s the largest deposits of high quality diamonds in the world were found in South Africa. Today Africa is the biggest source of diamonds. Botswana (in Africa) produces the most by value, but Russia the most by volume.

- Diamonds are the birthstone for April.
- Diamonds are the most expensive gemstones in the world!
- Diamonds are the hardest stones in the world!
- The largest cut diamond in the world is the Cullinan I (the First Star of Africa), it is 530 carats. It is set in the Sceptre, one of the British Crown Jewels.
- Amazing space fact: Star BPM 37093 in the constellation Centaurus is made from diamond (it is ten billion trillion trillion carats). It is nicknamed "Lucy" after the Beatles song "Lucy in the Sky with Diamonds".

Diamonds
The Most Precious Stone

Diamonds are used for jewellery and most famously for engagement rings (your mum may well have one). The first known diamond engagement ring was given in 1477 by Archduke Maxmillian of Austria to Mary of Burgundy – it was a gold ring featuring an M spelled out in diamonds.

The diamonds you see in rings or shops are cut from rough diamonds. Cut diamonds are valued based on the four Cs:- colour, clarity, carats and cut.

COLOUR: most diamonds appear colourless, but actually most "white diamonds" have slight yellow or brown tones. These "colours" are so slight that they are hard to see. The more colourless a white diamond is the more brilliance and sparkle it has; and the higher its value. Note: You can get pink, purple, green, black, blue and even red diamonds - because they are very rare these can be even more expensive.

CARAT: is the measure of a diamond's weight and by inference its size. The value of a diamond rises in proportion to its carat weight. The word carat comes from the Carob Tree whose seed was used for centuries as the standard for weighing precious stones. 1 carat = 0.2 grams. The average size of a diamond engagement ring is 0.75 carats.

CLARITY: is a measure of the natural marks and imperfections within a diamond. These marks come from tiny traces of minerals, gasses or other impurities and are called "inclusions". Clarity measures the number, size, location and nature of inclusions. Inclusions are generally invisible to the naked eye and each diamond is unique. The fewer inclusions, the higher the value. Flawless is the top grade of diamond, followed by Internally Flawless and the Very Very Slightly Included.

Most Popular Diamond Shapes /Cuts

CUT: how rough diamonds are cut determines how they reflect light and therefore their "brilliance" / sparkle. Cut refers to the facets (sides cut into the gem) not the shape. Most diamonds are cut round with 58 facets. The best quality cuts ensure the best sparkle and therefore price.

Finally there are many shapes that diamonds are cut into to make the most of the four C's; the most common are below.

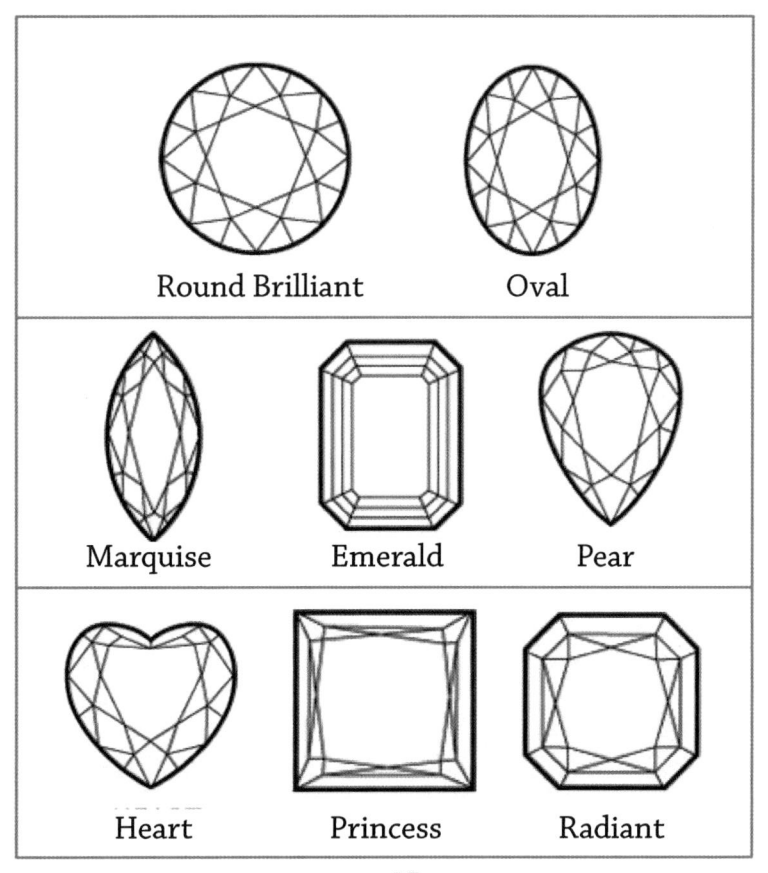

Round Brilliant	Oval
Marquise	Emerald	Pear
Heart	Princess	Radiant

February

March

September

October

Birthstones

Birthstones

Wearing birthstones dates from biblical times. By the 17th century certain stones had become associated with certain months; people would wear different stones each month. However in the 18th century people started to wear the stone associated with the month of their birth. Each stone has a meaning and both the stone and meaning can vary from country to country. Below are the UK birthstones (Note the stones are the same in the US but the meanings are different) .

JANUARY BIRTHSTONE GARNET (red). Garnet represents light, eternity, faith and truth.

FEBRUARY BIRTHSTONE AMETHYST (purple). Amethyst represents health, luck and wittiness.

MARCH BIRTHSTONE AQUAMARINE (pale blue) or bloodstone (dark green and red). Both represent happiness and understanding.

APRIL BIRTHSTONE DIAMOND (clear) or rock crystal (clear). Both represent eternity, courage and health.

MAY BIRTHSTONE EMERALD (deep green) or chrysoprase (pale green). Both represent fidelity, goodness and love.

JUNE BIRTHSTONE PEARL (white) or moonstone (white). Both represent beauty, nobility and peace.

JULY BIRTHSTONE RUBY (red) or carnelian (orangey red). Both represent enthusiasm, love and strength.

AUGUST BIRTHSTONE PERIDOT (pale green) or sardonyx (white & reddish brown). Both represent love, peace and success.

SEPTEMBER BIRTHSTONE SAPPHIRE (blue) or lapis lazuli (also blue). Both represent serenity and truth.

OCTOBER BIRTHSTONE OPAL (multi-coloured) or tourmaline. Both represents hope, health and purity.

NOVEMBER BIRTHSTONE TOPAZ (yellow) or citrine. Both represent courage, sincerity and wisdom.

DECEMBER BIRTHSTONE TURQUOISE (turquoise). Represents happiness, love and luck.

Alternatively ZODIAC SIGNS and days of the week also have gemstones associated with them.

Aquarius: garnet
Pisces: amethyst
Aries: bloodstone
Taurus: sapphire
Gemini: agate
Cancer: emerald
Leo: onyx
Virgo: carnelian
Libra: peridot
Scorpio: beryl
Sagittarius: topaz
Capricorn: ruby

Monday: pearl, crystal
Tuesday: ruby, emerald
Wednesday: amethyst, lodestone
Thursday: sapphire, carnelian
Friday: emerald, cat's eye
Saturday: turquoise, diamond
Sunday: topaz, diamond

Scotland

Land's End
The East Coast
Hebrides

Where to find Gemstones

Where to Find Gemstones in the UK

In the UK we are very lucky in that you can find many different types of gemstones naturally, particularly around our coastline. In fact you can get 15 types of gemstones, many of which you can find on beaches or in river beds. The map on the next page shows where you can find gemstones in the UK and Ireland.

Below is a list of gemstones found in the UK and Ireland and the symbol that is used on the map to mark where they are found.

- Agate
- Amethyst
- Amber
- Bloodstone
- Carnelian
- Chalcedony
- Cairngorm
- Flint
- Garnet
- Jasper
- Kyanite
- Quartz
- Serpentine
- Sapphire
- Topaz
- Zircon.

Next time you are on a pebble beach look out, you might find a rough gemstone.

To get an idea of how a stone will look if polished wet it.

UK Gemstone Map

Plus Shetland has amethyst, chalcedony and Kyanite

John o'Groats

Hebrides

Skye Marble

Scotland

North
West — East
South

Ireland

Wales

England

Land's End

65

Gemstone Checklist

Gemstone / Rock	Where found	Date
Agate		
Amethyst		
Amber		
Bloodstone		
Carnelian		
Chalcedony		
Cairngorm		
Flint		
Garnet		
Jasper		
Kyanite		
Quartz		
Serpentine		
Sapphire		
Topaz		
Zircon		

Printed in Great Britain
by Amazon